A Foot in the Door

A comedy

Richard Harris

Samuel French — London
www.samuelfrench-london.co.uk

FOR AMATEUR PRODUCTION ENQUIRIES

UNITED KINGDOM AND WORLD EXCLUDING NORTH AMERICA

plays@SamuelFrench-London.co.uk

020 7255 4302/01

Each title is subject to availability from Samuel French, depending upon country of performance.

A FOOT IN THE DOOR

First presented at the Mill at Sonning Dinner Theatre on 26th February 2003 with the following cast:

Warren Wallis	Ryan Romain
May Archer	Jacqueline Clarke
Desmond Donohoe	Derren Nesbitt
Stanislaw Stankowski	Harry Gostelow
Angela Assistant	Sally Geoghegan
Jilly Jordan	Kate Arneil

Directed by Sally Hughes
Set designed by Terry Parsons

CHARACTERS

Warren Wallis, a fledgling wardrobe salesman, black, young

May Archer, a widow, elderly

Desmond Donohoe, an experienced home security equipment salesman, late thirties

Stanislaw Stankowski (Stan), painter and decorator, Polish, mid-thirties

Angela Assistant, Stan's assistant, English, mid-thirties

Jilly Jordan, music keyboard saleswoman, early forties

SYNOPSIS OF SCENES

The action of the play takes place in the back sitting-room of May Archer's house, an outer London semi.

ACT I An early evening in summer

ACT II A few moments later

Time — the present

POLISH

Stan occasionally speaks in his native Polish. Translations and phonetic versions are given below.

Page 23:

Stan I need you I want you I love you.
Translation: Potrzebuje Cię chce Cię kocham Cię.
Phonetic version: Potcheboowye Cheyon htse Cheyon koham Cheyon.

Stan Let me take you, take you!
Translation: Oddaj mi się, oddaj się.
Phonetic version: Od-die mee sheyon, od-die sheyon.

Page 24:

Stan I'm going to make love to you, passionately, violently, until your eyes pop and your ears sing.
Translation: Będe kochał Cię y pasją, furią az ocyz Ci się, wybałuszą a w usłyszysz śpiew.
Phonetic version: Bownda kohow cheyon z pasyon, foorion, adj ochy Chi sheyon vybowushon a v ushac uswishish shpiev.

Page 47:

Stan I love you I need you I want you.
Translation: Kocham Cię potrzebuje Cię chce Cię.
Phonetic version: Koham Cheyon potcheboowye Cheyon htse Cheyon.

Page 48:

Stan I'm going to make you my own!
Translation: Posiąde Cię cała.
Phonetic version: Poshon-dey Cheyn tsawom.

The Polish translations and phonetic versions are by Janusz Ostrowski

Other plays by Richard Harris
published by Samuel French Ltd

Albert
The Business of Murder
Dead Guilty
Ghosts (adapted from J Basil Cowlishaw's translation
of the play by Henrik Ibsen)
In Two Minds
Is It Something I Said?
Local Affairs
The Maintenance Man
Outside Edge
Party Piece
Stepping Out
Stepping Out — The Musical (with lyrics by Mary Stewart-David
and music by Denis King)
Visiting Hour

ACT I

Early evening. The back sitting-room of an outer London semi. French windows give on to a small garden. The general décor and furnishings are old but immaculate. The most recent acquisition would be the large television set which is on but without sound

When the CURTAIN *rises Warren, a young black man in a stiff new suit, sits on the sofa, legs close together. On his knees is an open and very new document case. He is staring straight ahead, lips moving soundlessly. He is a fledgling salesman, out on his own for the first time, rehearsing his sales pitch by playing both parts. Every now and again he emits an audible "ah" — a little explosion of air by way of a nervous tic. He tells a joke and supplies his own Ted Heath raised shoulder soundless laughing response to it. But now his face is all-serious as he silently hardens the pitch, not seeing*

May, a senior citizen, comes in, straightening her Marks and Spencer dress

May That's better, now I can settle.

He immediately jumps to his feet, spilling the contents of his case over the floor. Apart from documents, they include an apple, a part-eaten sandwich and bottle of water. So that he is on his hands and knees collecting the contents as May sits in her chair, with:

May Which one are you again, dear? Sorry.
Warren Sorry?
May I've forgotten which one you are. (*Her eyes have gone to the silent television set from which they will seldom stray throughout:*)
Warren Which one I am. Sorry?
May Are you windows or are you wardrobes?

He takes a moment to follow her meaning

Warren Oh — right — wardrobes.
May Only I think I might have asked the man to come round about the windows. You're not him, then.
Warren No — wardrobes — I telephoned for an appointment — ah!

May I know you did, dear, it's not you, it's me, I get confused, especially with dates, that's why I write it all down on a little piece of paper only I can't find it. Mind you, when I do find it I can't find my glasses.

Warren (*pleased to have a point of contact*) *I* used to wear glasses.

May Oh yes dear?

Warren Now I wear contact lenses. Well, one. I'm saving up for the other one. You'd never know, would you? (*He offers his eye for examination*)

May What colour is it?

Warren Green.

May No offence but it looks more maroon.

Warren That's because it hasn't settled in properly, I've only had it a week.

May Well it'll look really natural once it's stopped watering I'm sure it will.

Warren Thank you.

May D'you know where I found them last time?

Warren What? Sorry?

May My glasses.

Warren No?

May In the butter dish in the fridge.

Warren Wow.

May That's what happens when you get older, you forget things. Mind you, my sister said I was always the same. She would though. Fancied herself rotten she did, just cos she did a bit of reading. Do you read?

Warren I used to when I was younger.

May I like the Daily Mail I must admit and the TV Times, I like the TV Times, it gives you all the information — but her — read read read, that's all she did. Her husband worked in the crematorium so she was on her own a lot.

Warren Oh yes?

May My hubby was in haulage, God rest his soul. (*Of the television*) Look at the state of her skin. She's not eating properly I know she isn't. (*And again her attention is fully on the television*)

Warren waits. She would seem to have forgotten his existence. He does a quick run-through of his opening spiel and launches into:

Warren May I say how delighted I am that you have chosen The Wonderful World Of Wardrobes to further enhance this already delightful property.

May My nephew was a salesman, you know.

Warren Oh yes?

May He sold hearing aids. Trouble was, when he knocked at the door they couldn't hear him.

Warren works it out and:

Warren As you know, bedrooms come in many shapes and sizes but fortunately so does the large range of designs in our collection. Over two hundred robes and associated pieces are available in a choice of up to eight finishes, each piece beautifully-designed and finished in easy care synthetic laminate. Furthermore, I am pleased to tell you that, should you decide to go ahead with our amazing current offer, you will automatically receive either a complete body makeover or a weekend in Belgium.

May Oh that's nice. (*And she turns to look at him, pleased with herself*) Here, d'you know who you remind me of?

Warren Sorry?

May I've been trying to think who you remind me of.

Warren Oh yes?

May That boy in what's-its-name …you know — what's-his-name — the one out of whatsit … (*She waves a finger at the television*) … the one who left his wife for what's-her-name, the one with the big nose and the speech defect … *Julian.*

Warren Oh.

May It's the quiff.

Warren I haven't got a quiff. (*But unsure what a quiff is*) Have I?

May No I mean if you did have.

Warren Yes. Ah! (*Under his breath to himself*) Only the positives, only the positives … (*and, brightly*) … as I understand it, you spoke to one of our telesales executives.

May That's right, dear, yes, this woman phoned up. We had a really nice conversation.

Warren As a result of which… (*He checks, thinking it through*) And as a result of this really nice telephone conversation you were sent a copy of our latest catalogue.

May I was, dear, yes.

Warren Which you no doubt found very helpful.

May There, look, you can see her bones showing. Found what very helpful?

Warren (*thinks about it*) Our latest catalogue.

May Oh yes, very helpful.

Warren Excellent. Ah!

May I said to my son when he phoned, they've sent me this catalogue and it's just the job it is.

Warren Would that be in terms of the layout or the general information?

May In terms of what, dear?

Warren The words or the pictures.

May No dear, no. The thickness.

Warren The thickness.

May Just the job that was.

Warren How d'you mean? Sorry. Ah!

May To stop the table wobbling. (*She indicates*) That leg's been trouble ever since Lady Diana died Oo-er, no disrespect.

Warren No, I agree, she was a lovely person.

May No, I mean your whatsit. (*She indicates*) My son, my David, said he'd get me a new one but I said what do I want with a new table I'm quite happy with this one thankyou and besides, you've got enough on your plate. Well they would have, they've just moved to Croydon.

Warren Oh yes?

May Yes. They've got trams, you know.

Warren So I understand, yes.

May Where does it run to? Oh yes, whatsit, where they have the tennis. Whatsit

Warren Wimbledon.

May Wimbledon. Going on about it like it's something that's just been invented but they had trams when *I* was a girl. Dirty big things they were with sparks flying everywhere, my little frocks used to get filthy. Mind you, dear, it's all the same, isn't it? Nothing changes, does it, all you've got to do is sit still and everything comes round again … frocks, hairdos, trams, everything. That's him, getting his diploma. (*She indicates a photograph*) My David.

Warren Oh. (*He raises impressed eyebrows in the direction of the photograph and has to quickly adjust his lens which seems to be shifting, then turns back to her, smiling wildly*)

She smiles back and looks at the television. It's as though he isn't there. This moment. Warren sitting with a fixed smile which slowly fades and:

Excuse me.

May What's that, dear?

Warren What I would like to do is take some measurements so that I shall be able to provide you with an idea of what we're talking about. (*He holds up the steel tape measure he has taken from his case*)

May I thought we were talking about windows.

Warren Wardrobes. In terms of price. We are as you know at the very top of the range.

May You'll need something to stand on then.

Warren Would that be convenient? (*He has taken out a notepad and ballpoint*)

May What's that dear?

Warren For me to go upstairs and take measurements of your bedroom.

May Course it is — don't stand on the bed though, will you, not unless you take your shoes off.

Warren Would you like to accompany me?

May My hubby used to play the piano accordion. We had some lovely Christmasses in the old days.

Warren I was thinking in terms of your peace of mind in terms of me being alone that is unchaperoned. Upstairs.

May No dear no you go and enjoy yourself while I have a look at my programme — they're getting married because he wants children and this is the episode where she's faced with telling him about her internals.

There is a brisk ring at the doorbell. It makes Warren jump

See who that is for me, will you dear? If it's a man with a message from God, tell him thankyouverymuch but I had one *last* week. (*She points the remote control at the television*)

The sound comes up. A soap opera. Lots of domestic disharmony

Warren stands for a moment, unsure, and then

Warren Right. Right. Err…

A moment, and he goes out, taking his briefcase

May is totally engrossed in the television, like he was never there

May (*to the television*) Oh I say, the things she says. (*She leans closer*) Don't you believe a word of it, Michael, she's wicked that one.

Warren comes in, followed by Desmond. Desmond is thickset, an experienced salesman in his late 30s. He wears a good if somewhat sharp suit, a tie in broad red and yellow stripes, carries a large silver metal case, a mobile telephone and a tiny tape recorder

Warren (*referring to a card and announcing:*) Err… Desmond Donohoe Samson Home Security. (*He has wrongly stressed the second syllable in Donohoe*)

Desmond (*correcting him*) Donohoe. (*He sets down the case*) Good evening, Mrs Archer. (*He has a light Southern Irish accent and appears to be brimming with confidence*)

May Are you windows?

Warren (*getting it right*) Donohoe.

Desmond Windows, doors, you name it good lady, we protect it. A Samson Home Is A Secure Home. (*He takes the card and puts it in Warren's pocket as:*)

Desmond Who did you say you were again?
Warren Warren Wallis, The Wonderful World Of Wardrobes..
Desmond Can you verify that?
Warren You're not the only one with a card.
Desmond Then where is it?
Warren (*producing a card*) Here.

Desmond takes the card and looks at it and

Desmond How many L's in Wallis?
Warren Two.
Desmond Mm (*He returns the card as*) I am right, am I not, Mrs Archer, we
did say half seven.
May It's my fault, I get confused.

Warren has been looking at his card, having trouble focussing

Warren And she can't find her glasses — (*to May*)I'll just pop upstairs then
— ah!
May That's right, dear, oo-er, look at the state of her kitchen.
Warren (*pointedly*) Then I'll come down with my measurements and we
can continue our interesting and mutually beneficial discussion.

He goes out, taking his briefcase, and having trouble with his contact lens

Desmond closes the door after him and launches into:

Desmond What a very lovely home you have, Mrs Archer. A very lovely
home but sadly not in a very lovely world which is why of course I am here.
Desmond Donohoe, Samson Home Security. You'll be wanting to see my
ID. (*He holds up his ID card and photograph for her to see, setting his face
alongside it in matching stern mode*)
May Very nice, dear, come and sit yourself down.
Desmond Thank you. (*He sits, hitching up his trousers, and we see that he
is wearing one red sock and one yellow, in tones that match his tie.
Throughout the following he will touch the knot of his tie and then do a
considerable amount of leg-acting to draw attention to the socks*)

May remains apparently oblivious

May I say … where did you park your horse?
Desmond Which horse would that be now?
May My hubby always used to say wherever you find an Irishman, you'll
find a horse.

Desmond A man of the turf, was he?
May He did like his little flutter.
Desmond How did he go?
May Oh he didn't travel, he watched it on the telly.
Desmond I mean his passing.
May I took him up a cuppa tea and when I went back half an hour later it was stone cold and so was he.
Desmond Tragic, tragic … (*He brings his case closer, ready for use with:*) Mrs Archer …

There is a brisk knock on the door and Warren comes in

Warren Excuse me.
May What's that, dear?
Warren Which one is it, sorry.
May Which one is it what, dear?
Warren Bedroom — ah!
May The one in the front with the pink eiderdown.
Warren Thank you. (*He makes to go but:*)
May (*of the television*) You see her? She used to be married to that what's-his-name out of the other one.
Desmond I do believe you're right.
Warren He's the one with the quiff.
May No, dear, no, that's the other one.

Desmond smirks

Warren exits

May I expect it's his eyes — one of them hasn't settled in yet.

Desmond has closed the door

Desmond Mrs Archer, you recently completed a telephone survey in which you expressed an interest in having your home properly secured. Which is why I am here — to offer you, free of charge, a comprehensive consultancy regarding the security of your lovely home — as I say, a lovely home in an unlovely world.
May My sister used to live in Peckham.
Desmond Do you know what I said to myself, the moment I saw you?
May What's that dear?
Desmond I said to myself, this is a very trusting person. That's all part of the job, you see: to sum up people. To instantly evaluate the nature of the person with whom one is dealing.

May Oh yes?

Desmond If I had to sum you up in one word the word I would use is trusting.

May My late sister always said I was shifty.

Desmond Then with all respect to your sister, I would say she was quite mistaken

May She said I never look anyone in the eye. She said I look at people's noses.

Desmond You can tell a lot about people by their nose.

May And their eyelashes.

Desmond And their eyelashes.

May Never trust a man with ginger eyelashes. Mind you, that Michael Caine's done all right for himself.

Desmond Hasn't he just — but you follow my gist.

May Not really dear no.

Desmond You are a widow. A very trusting lady, living alone.

May My son comes over every other Wednesday.

Desmond He sounds like a very loving human being.

May Well he would do if he wasn't so busy.

Desmond I don't want to distress you, far be it from me to distress you, but I visited a lady the other night — the last time I saw her she was a rosy-cheeked little grandmother of six sitting in a chair knitting pullovers for illegal immigrants and humming along to Radio Three — now she is a vegetable and not only is she a vegetable, she is a penniless vegetable. Both she and her lovely home had been violated by a pitiless intruder and what happens? The insurance company quibbles over the small print and why? Because of her lack of security. You tell your insurance company you are dealing with me and your premiums will plummet. (*Into tape recorder*) Advise client of alternative insurance cover, special terms as applicable. (*And instantly back again*) I tell you this story not to frighten you but to make you aware and I thank God, I thank God, that He pointed you in the direction of Samson Home Security.

May The woman at number 28 was a religious maniac.

Desmond Is that right?

May She used to have visions. Mind you, they never had a telly so I suppose she had to have something to look at.

Desmond If I may take you back.

May Where to, dear?

Desmond To the war

May You mean Hitler?

Desmond I do.

May I don't care *what* they say, dog lover or no dog lover, that man was a rotter.

Desmond People imagine that during the war there was no crime against person or property because we were all pulling together. But peruse your local newspaper records and you will see that little old ladies such as your goodself were the victims of ration book bandits, coal thieves, cinema molestation, foreign servicemen, you name it.

May My sister went out with a Yank who knew Ronald Coleman. Well he said he knew him only we found out he was a pastry cook in the Highland Light Infantry.

Desmond That's it, you see. Deception. All is deception. Take me for example. Who am I?

May You're the man from the thingy.

Desmond That's who I *say* I am because that's how they work, these people —they inveigle their way into your home by dint of a pleasing personality. I could turn nasty at any minute.

May My cousin Fred turned nasty. It depended where the moon was.

Desmond However ... with the 24 hour wraparound protection provided by Samson Home Security ...

There is a knock and Warren comes in

Warren All done and a very lovely room if I might say so.

Desmond Take for example this young man here. Who did he say he was again?

May Who did you say you were again, dear?

Warren Warren Wallis The Wonderful World Of Wardrobes.

Desmond (*into the recorder*) Immediate action, run security check on Wonderful World Of Windows representative Warren Wallis, one L.

Warren Two and it's Wardrobes.

Desmond Tell me this, Mrs Archer: how do you know that he and I are not in cahoots?

May In where dear?

Desmond How do you know that while I've been down here keeping you talking young Warren hasn't been upstairs putting his fingers into everything that you hold sacred?

Warren Excuse me ...

Desmond ... of course you haven't, Warren, of course you haven't ... (*giving May a gentle jolly nudge*) ... at least we assume he hasn't, eh Mrs Archer? (*His face immediately serious again*) I am so glad, I am so glad you contacted me. Your peace of mind ... is my peace of mind. Now what I would like to do — with your permission of course is to go outside and study your premises from the criminal point of view — starting at the rear.

May All right dear yes.

Desmond Thank you. Through here, is it?

May Through the kitchen, yes dear.

Desmond Thank you. (*He makes to go but:*)
May I say ... you wouldn't mind doing me a bit of a favour while you're out there, would you? (*She beckons him closer*)

He returns to bend so that she can speak into his ear

Desmond What's that? (*He smirks at Warren*)
May I've left a bit of washing on the line, you couldn't bring it in for me, could you, dear?

The smirk disappears

Desmond Always a pleasure, never a chore. (*To Warren*) By the time I've done that you'll no doubt have completed your business and have gone on your way. (*He moves away but stops at the door and makes a show of examining it with:*) Look at this door, a child could get through this door, let alone a maniac with a pickaxe, no substance, no substance whatsoever. (*He speaks into his recorder*) Special attention downstairs doors, suggest QB over four double-stressed with co-lateral hinging.

He goes out

May Doesn't he talk nice?

Warren has been dabbing his sore eye. He takes a catalogue from his briefcase as:

Warren If I might ask ... which of our comprehensive range most took your fancy?
May What's that dear?
Warren (*indicating the catalogue*) Wardrobes.
May Well I hadn't thought about it really.
Warren Oh. Ah!
May What do *you* think?
Warren (*thrown*) Umm ... well, definitely something traditional.
May Oh yes I like traditional.
Warren (*seizing the positive*) You like traditional.
May Oh yes I'm all for traditional. I mean, you think when old Winston went. Beautiful that was, all them cranes dipping and the horses with their muffled hooves and everything. Beautiful.

Warren opens his mouth but realizes that he doesn't know what to say

Desmond appears outside the french windows, ostensibly checking them for security as he talks into his recorder but with an eye very much on Warren

Warren becomes aware of Desmond and snaps into:

Warren Excellent, yes, an excellent choice if I might say so — yes — here we are — pages thirteen to twenty two, our Adelphi, Connaught and West Wittering range, each offering fourteen robes of great versatility in a choice of either antique Florentine finish or simulated hardwood, distressed, lacquered and handwaxed to a golden sheen. Are we talking single robe or double?

May What do *you* think?

Warren I think we are talking single.

May I think you're right.

Warren A single robe with perhaps a matching six drawer tallboy and open shelf unit or, if you prefer, the large bedroom chest with deep bottom drawer which, with its easyrun castors is perfect for both storage and ease of accessibility.

Desmond exits

Warren looks at the french windows and is relieved to see that Desmond is no longer there. So he can relax a bit

Warren What do you think then?

May What do I think what, dear?

Warren We have to decide, you see.

May Oh I don't make decisions, dear.

Warren You don't make decisions.

May No, dear, no, never have done. (*Of the telly*) Is that thingy out of whatsit? Oh no, it's the other one.

An awful thought is occurring to Warren

Warren Without wishing to be — er — it is you to whom I should be speaking to. Whom.

May How d'you mean, dear? (*Of the telly*) Yes, it is him, look.

Warren What I mean is … you did say there is no *Mr* Archer. In terms of a husband.

May Oh I see what you mean. No dear no, he passed on five years ago, bless him. You'd think they'd give her a different apron, wouldn't you, she had that one on last week.

Warren So that it will be your signature on the agreement should we come to one. When we come to one. Agreement. Ah!

May Oh I don't sign things. Not any more. I used to, I used to be very good at it til my sister stuck her nose in as per. You're always signing things, she used to say, well I like signing things I said and d'you know what she said? She said the only thing you should be signing is the back of a prescription. Oh look, here they are, I've been sitting on them. (*She holds up a pair of National Health specs*)

Desmond comes in with a plastic basket full of washing

Desmond All done and if I might say so, in the nick of time. (*Into his recorder*) Repeat: fortify all points of entry, top priority, top priority.
Warren Would you mind if I made a quick call to head office?
May (*of her phone*) Help yourself, dear.
Warren No, that's all right, thank you ... (*He holds up his mobile*) ... I'll umm I'll do it outside if you don't mind.

He goes out with his briefcase

May (*of her glasses*) I've been sitting on them.
Desmond So you have (*Of the washing*) Where will I put this?
May Put it on the side, will you, dear, I like to do my ironing in front of the telly.
Desmond Will I put it here?
May That's lovely.

He sets the washing down and:

Desmond Now then, Mrs Archer, here's what I propose.
May I tell you what, dear, I'm just going to make a nice cup of tea. (*She struggles to her feet*)

Desmond aids her

Nice cup of tea and a digestive, you'd like that, I know you would. (*She makes to go out but:*)
May What did you say your name was again?
Desmond Donohoe, Desmond Donohoe. (*He adjusts his tie and hoiks up his trousers, revealing the odd socks*)
May Our old milkman was called Donohoe. You're no relation by any chance?
Desmond Not that I'm aware of.
May No disrespect but they were a funny lot. They kept chickens under their kitchen table.
Desmond Well I never.
May In the end we had to get the council round. There was a lot of ill-feeling of course but as my hubby said to them, how would *you* like it if *I* had a cock that woke *you* up at four o'clock every morning?

She goes out

He stands. Then takes up the remote control, turns down the sound on the television, puts down the remote control, then on second thoughts hides it under the sofa, then pulls out his mobile, sits, and dials urgently. As he does he is unaware that:

Warren has appeared in the garden, to pace to and fro, using his mobile and still holding his case

Desmond waits for the phone to be answered. For the first time he is exhibiting insecurity

Desmond Not the answerphone, please, not the answerphone … (*He waits, in some anguish for the answerphone message to end*)

Warren, phone to ear, peers at Desmond through the window. Desmond sees him and immediately both men put on big smiles and mime positive phone talk

Warren goes out of sight and:

Desmond (*immediately*) Laura, it's me. I know you're there please pick up the phone. Please? (*He waits*) All right all right … I know you're angry with me, I know things are bad, I know just lately I haven't been the best husband in the world but it's all going to change, I promise you. Tonight I'm bringing you home a wonderful surprise, a chance for us to start all over again … I know you're there, Laura, please talk to me …

But Warren comes in and immediately Desmond changes tone

… so that's a close on number 231, a close on number 482 and I shall shortly be closing on this one, number 637. What's that, my lovely? No no, just type out the order forms and leave them on my desk with all the others. You're a darling. (*He blows a kiss into the mobile and switches off. Actually, he'd switched off as soon as Warren came in*)
Desmond All right?
Warren I'm all right, are you all right?
Desmond Couldn't be better. Could not be better.

This moment. Each wishing the other would clear off out of it

Warren The lady's making a cup of tea.
Desmond She said, yes.

The moment continues until:

Desmond First time out on your own, is it?
Warren (*defensively*) No.
Desmond Are you sure now?
Warren Course I am.
Desmond Twenty years, me.
Warren Yeah?
Desmond You name it, I've sold it.
Warren (*a trump card*) You've got odd socks on.
Desmond I have (*And what's more he shows them*) You'll remember me, won't you? The man in the odd socks.
Warren I will, yes.
Desmond And so will the customer. (*He mimes phoning*) "Hello Mrs Archer, Desmond Donohoe here". "I'm sorry, dear, which one are you, I see so many" "The one in the odd socks and the matching neckwear". (*He touches his tie knot*) Straightaway she knows me. We have contact.
Warren (*impressed*) That's good, that is.
Desmond You've a receptive mind.
Warren Thank you.
Desmond But do you use it?
Warren Err...
Desmond Do you believe in yourself? Do you look in the mirror and pump yourself up every morning?
Warren Not in the mirror I don't, no.
Desmond Show me a good salesman and I'll show you a man with large testicles. (*He stands, legs apart*)
Warren I do all right in that department thankyouverymuch. (*He stands likewise*)
Desmond Can I give you a little tip, a little *entrée*?
Warren (*shrugging*) Go on then.
Desmond As soon as you walk into the room, you quietly drop a twenty pound note on the floor. (*He does so*) So you're talking away, nice and friendly, not on to the pitch yet, and suddenly you "notice" this twenty pound note. This must be yours, you say, holding it out to the client ... (*which he does now*) ... oh I don't think so, says the client, I think it must be yours, it must have fallen out of your wallet when you were giving me your card. Are you sure, you say? Quite sure, says he and you do a little bit more to-ing and fro-ing and finally he persuades you to put the money in your wallet which you do with suitable reluctance and what is he thinking? He is thinking this is an honest man, this is a man I can do business with.

Warren thinks about it and:

Warren Does it have to be a twenty?
Desmond A ten will do but nothing less. What do you know about body
  language?
Warren I borrowed a book on it
Desmond Do you look the customer directly in the eye?
Warren I will when I've got my other lens in.
Desmond Let me feel your handshake.

They shake hands

  That's it, is it, that's your handshake.
Warren What's wrong with it?
Desmond You don't mind getting a few tips, do you?
Warren Depends who from.
Desmond From someone at the very top of the tree.
Warren (*risking it*) The higher the monkey climbs the tree, the more you
  can see of its arse.
Desmond Make your point.
Warren I'm just saying. Ah!
Desmond All right, you're a quick learner, but tell me, do you know your
  Kipling?
Warren Err...
Desmond   "I keep six honest serving men,
        They taught me all I knew,
        Their names are What and Why and When
        And How and Where and Who."
  Say it with me one two three ...

*And he repeats the lines, conducting Warren who joins in with growing
confidence*

Warren I like that. Thank you.
Desmond Fail to plan and you're planning to fail.
Warren I know that.
Desmond What is it then?
Warren What?
Desmond Your plan, your platform, your initial approach, your hook.
Warren Umm.
Desmond The minute you come through that door, you have to have a
  platform, something upon which to build.

Warren I know what a platform is, thank you.

Desmond Do you know what my platform is?

Warren Go on then.

Desmond Fear.

Warren Fear?

Desmond The customer is frightened of her house being broken into. I am confirming the basis for her fears and therefore her need to protect herself with my product. The greater the fear, the greater the need.

Warren But she's an old lady.

Desmond Which is why before you know it I've replaced that fear with confidence. She has confidence in me therefore she will have confidence in my product QED. Let me tell you something, Warren.

Warren Excuse me, you haven't stopped.

Desmond (*putting an avuncular arm around him*) I feel that in the last few minutes you and I have become very close. And because of that, I am going to take you into my confidence.

Warren Oh yes?

Desmond Yes. (*The arm on the shoulder becomes a little more aggressive*) This is a very important sale for me — probably the most important sale I'll ever make now you'd be doing me a great favour if you went on your way and let me get on with it. So sod off, will you?

Warren Excuse me ...

May comes in, digging into her handbag

May You'll never guess what's happened.

Warren ⎫
      ⎬ (*together*) No?
Desmond ⎭

May I've run out of biscuits.

Warren ⎫
      ⎬ (*together*) Oh dear.
Desmond ⎭

May We can't have a cuppa tea without a nice biscuit, can we?

Warren ⎫
      ⎬ (*together*) Umm.
Desmond ⎭

May Now who's going to be a good boy and pop down to the corner for me?

Desmond (*cheerily*) Off you go then, Warren.

Warren Why me?

Desmond Why not?

Warren What sort?

May Some nice digestives — here you are, dear, five pounds, that's all I've got.

Warren Anything else or just the biscuits?

May Just the biscuits, thank you, dear.

Warren looks at Desmond who jerks his head — shove off — and goes out

May sits, looks at the television

May What's happened to the sound?
Desmond I've no idea.
May We can't sit here with no sound, can we, where's my plunger?

She will look for the remote control as

Desmond Well I've had a look outside, Mrs Archer, and … (*Then, as though he's been dying to say it all evening*) … I have to tell you this: you remind me so much of my dear old auntie Kate.
May I can't find my thingy. My whatsit. My plunger. (*She mimes and searches the cushions*)
Desmond Oh she was a lovely woman, lovely. Looking at you now is like she'd never gone away. (*This as May is bending over the arm of the sofa, her behind to him*) You'd make a soft-hearted fellah very happy if just for this evening you let me call you auntie.
May (*upright again*) You're a bit of an old sprucer, you are.
Desmond That's as maybe but I guarantee my heart's in the right place.
May Say that again.
Desmond (*a little bit more of the Oirish twinkle*) That's as maybe but I guarantee my heart's in the right place.
May Here — do you know who you remind me of?
Desmond (*knowing full well*) Who would that be now?
May That what's-his-name. (*She grits her teeth and revolves her hands in frustration*)
Desmond (*singing*) "I'm only a strolling vagabond…"
May That's him!

Desmond has knelt and taken her hand

Desmond (*singing*) "So good-night pretty lady … goo-ood-night"
May You've got a really lovely voice.
Desmond So they say.
May I used to love a bit of a sing-song.
Desmond I'll get you an invitation to the rugby club — would you like that, auntie?
May My hubby had a lovely voice. A mixture of Fats Domino and Dicky Valentine. Christmas time he used to black up and do *The Sheik Of Araby*.
Desmond (*singing, quietly, with a bit of hand movement*) "I'm The Sheik Of Araby"

May (*delighted*) You know it.
Desmond Know it? I love it.
May You and my hubby would have got on really well.
Desmond You must miss him something terrible.
May I do. Even if he did have a reclining forehead.

He holds his understanding look. But now stands purposefully and:

Desmond But to the purpose of my visit: I've had a look round from the
outside and the first thing that occurs ...
May My sister couldn't sing for toffee.
Desmond No?
May Not a note.
Desmond Amazing.
May D'you know what they used to call us?
Desmond Who's that?
May Me and my sister.
Desmond (*twinkly*) Betty Grable and Alice Faye.
May Stewed Prunes And Apple Tart.
Desmond Is that right?
May (*shaping her mouth into a tight little hole*) Stewed Prunes ... that was
her ... (*now letting the mouth go large and loose as:*) and Apple Tart ... that
was me. Her all posh and me all common, saucy cow.
Desmond As I was saying. I've had a look outside and ...
May ... she used to live here, you know.
Desmond Who did?
May My sister.
Desmond Oh?
May Oh yes. Her hubby expired just after mine did and my son, my David,
said why don't you move in together, keep each other company, so she
come to live here, her being in a rented place with only the one bedroom
and then blow me last year *she* goes and dies so I'm on my own again, that's
why he got me a new telly, my David, twenty-six inch this is but I'll tell you
this, if it was her sitting here instead of me you wouldn't be getting much
out of her, I mean *I've* always liked a bit of company, a nice conversation,
but her, she was always close, her mouth was drawn with a very thin nib,
I can tell you.

There is a ring at the front door

May That was quick, let him in for me, will you, dear?
Desmond (*opening his mouth to protest, but:*) Always a pleasure, never a
chore.

He goes out

She resumes her search for the remote control. Unable to find it, she thumps the television in an attempt to get sound out of it

Desmond comes in

Desmond (*stunned*) It's the man about the decorating.
May Oh yes, dear, what decorating is that?
Desmond I don't know, I don't know. (*To the door*) What decorating is that?

Stan comes in. He is tall, very thin, cadaverous. He wears a cheap blue and white baseball cap, a cheap bulbous bomber jacket and very tight jeans that all in all give him the appearance of an ostrich. His right arm is in a narrow sling

Stan Put card in letter box. (*He mimes how he did so*)
Desmond (*suspiciously, to impress May*) What did it say, this card?
Stan Say Stanislaw Stankowski, Painting Paperhanging And Plastering No Job Too Small. (*He holds out his card*)

Desmond takes it and examines it closely as:

Give personal undertaking you receive honest advice, proper specification and satisfactory conclusion. (*To May*) I say give you quotation.
May Oh — yes — that's right, I remember now — (*to Desmond*) — he was putting it in the box just as I was going out to clean my step — we had a nice chat, didn't we, dear?
Stan You say pop in whenever convenient.
May Course I did — sit yourself down.
Stan Thank you. Prefer stand.
Desmond (*into his recorder, reading the card*) Immediate action security check on Stanislaw Stankowski, Painter And Decorator (*He looks up at Stan*) Do you have any identification?
Stan Have season ticket to Queens Park Rangers.
Desmond May I see it please?

The doorbell rings

May Who's that?
Stan Is assistant.
Desmond Assistant?
Stan Because of injured hand, assistant necessary write down measurement. (*He indicates his bandaged arm*)

May Let him in, will you, dear?

Desmond opens his mouth to protest but:

Desmond Certainly, certainly.

He goes out

Stan In Poland, we make finest jam in whole world.
May I bet you say that to all the girls.
Stan No, say because believe you are lady with whom I can be completely sincere.
May Oh I say!

Angela comes in. She is short, wears similar clothing to Stan's, but her jeans are baggy. Her long hair is pulled up under a cap and she wears dark glasses. She carries a notebook

Angela (*over-brightly*) Good evening! Which of you gentlemen is Mr Stankowski?
Stan Speaking.

Desmond has come in and will eye them suspiciously as:

Angela We've never met, you see.
Stan Never!
Angela The agency sent me.
Stan Agency, yes.
Angela Shall we commence then, Mr Stankowski?
Desmond One moment. (*He leans close to May*) In view of our little bit of business, auntie, I suggest you ask them to come back tomorrow.

Angela gives a gasp of horror

Angela I can't I can't!
Stan Tomorrow impossible.
May That's what he calls me — auntie.
Stan (*assertively*) Who are you?
Desmond (*equally assertively*) Who am *I*?
May He's an old sprucer, that's who he is.
Angela Might I ask what is his capacity?
May He's from wardrobes.
Desmond Windows. And all other points of entry. (*Giving cards to Stan and Angela*) Desmond Donohoe, Samson Home Security.

Angela (*fearfully*) Security?
Desmond A Samson Home Is A Secure Home. (*He touches his tie and shows his socks*)
Stan Have question.
Desmond Fire away.
Stan Is OK to leave ladder on top of van?
Desmond Is ladder secured?
Stan Is tied.
Desmond Is rope?
Stan Is string.
Desmond Is no good.
Stan Is only ladder.
Desmond Is your problem.
Stan (*to May*) Is OK put in garden?
May Help yourself, dear.

Stan and Angela go out

May I wish I could find my plunger. (*She mimes pointing the remote control at the television*)

Desmond looks at his watch, his nerves starting to fray, but he steadies himself and:

Desmond What I could do, you see auntie, is offer you steel-reinforced doors fitted with an 18 bolt locking system and capable of withstanding a three hour assault with a crow bar and pickaxe but I don't think that's what you're looking for
May No dear I'm looking for my plunger.
Desmond I *could* suggest our automatically activated Monsoon Marvel spray system which squirts intruders with a solution containing a unique forensic code that remains detectable on skin for weeks and clothing indefinitely.
May My hubby got sprayed once by a passing bus and it wasn't even raining.
Desmond I could also suggest turning your *en suite* bathroom into a panic room with independent power supply, blast proof door and smoke barrier system, but that would involve over four hundred metres of cable and a great deal of carpet-lifting which I think to a home-loving lady such as your goodself would be far too disturbing.
May The woman at number sixty-three was disturbed. In the end they had to give her a cerstificate. Her husband went off with a mobile chiropodist so it was a relief all round really.
Desmond So what I am going to suggest, auntie, what I am going to suggest

and what I know will bring you not only the maximum peace of mind but also the minimum amount of disruption is … (*He triumphantly holds up the silver case*)… The Cyclops Three Thousand.

Warren comes in with a packet of biscuits

Warren There's someone in your garden with a ladder.

May That's all right, dear, he's from Poland.

Warren Here we are then: your biscuits and your change from *ten pounds*.

May I thought I gave you five.

Warren No, it was definitely *ten pounds*.

May Oh well dear if you say so (*She takes the biscuits and the money from him and makes for the door with:*) I'll put the kettle on again and we can all have a nice cup of tea. I tell you what, dear, you wouldn't like to have a look for my plunger, would you?

She mimes using her plunger and goes

Warren stares down at the hand from which she took the money, then up at Desmond

Warren Might I have a word?

Desmond Excuse *me (And he goes out with his case and:*)As I was saying, auntie — the Cyclops Closed Circuit System, as recently endorsed by The Duke and Duchess of Wessex.

Desmond exits

Warren Ah! (*He sits, trying to work it out*)

Stan and Angela come in

Warren immediately stands

Stan Is up against wall.

Warren Excuse me who are you?

Stan Stankowski, Painting Paperhanging and Plastering — No Job Too Small. (*He gives Warren a card*)

Angela There are further details available on his website.

Stan www. Stanstan.co.uk.

Angela Alternatively, you may call his number twenty four hours a day for prompt attention, not including Sundays.

Warren Who are you?

Angela I am Mr Stankowski's assistant.

Stan Who are *you*?

Warren Warren Wallis, The Wonderful World of Wardrobes. (*He passes his card*)

Angela takes it and will read it as:

Stan Wardrobes.

Warren Might you be interested in a wardrobe?

Stan Whole world interested in wardrobe.

Warren (*brightly seizing the moment*) In that case let me show you our catalogue.

Angela In what case?

Warren In this case. (*He bends as though to open his case but:*) Oh look. A ten-pound note. You must have dropped it.

Stan Thank you. (*He takes the note and pockets it*)

Warren's face drops. He looks from his empty hand to Stan

Warren Will you excuse me a moment?

He goes out, taking his case

Stan and Angela remain frozen. Then Stan moves to close the door and

Stan (*in Polish*) I need you I want you I love you.

Angela Oh Stan, Stan…this is madness, madness!

Stan (*in Polish*) Let me take you, take you!

Angela From the moment we met you have reduced me to a puddle of mixed emotion … one half of me riddled with guilt, the other half unable to resist your naked animal attraction … wherever, whenever — I must have you!

Stan Angela, Angela …

Angela Stan, Stan … (*She pulls off the glasses and the cap so that her hair cascades down*)

They rush into each other's arms, Stan removing his right arm from the sling as they do. They kiss passionately

May comes in, humming "The Sheik Of Araby"

Immediately they jerk apart. Now Stan is wearing his left arm in the sling. Angela rams the cap back on her head, the glasses on her nose and gets her small pad and pencil at the ready. Stan extends a metre of steel tape measure and holds it against a wall

Stan Thirteen point seven six. (*He lets the tape roll back*) Minimum ten roll five litre.

Angela duly makes a note of this as:

Angela Ten roll five litre.
Stan Prefer gloss or eggshell?
May What's that, dear?
Angela Paint.
May I don't mind really, dear, just as long as it's a nice colour.
Stan (*pointing at Angela*) Make note: nice colour.
Angela Nice … colour.
May Now what did I want to ask you? Oh yes, do you drink tea or being continental do you prefer coffee, because if you do I haven't got none of that decapitated.
Stan Thank you. Tea is good.
Angela Sadly we don't have the time, do we Stan ... kowski, Mister.
Stan No. No time. Must do what come here to do. (*To Angela, in Polish*) I'm going to make love to you, passionately, violently, until your eyes pop and your ears sing.

Angela gives a little scream of sexual pleasure

Angela Yes, yes, yes!
May Oh, you've changed your mind then, have you, dear?
Stan
            } (*together*) No, no, no!
Angela
May Are you sure, the pair of you?

They ad lib their certainty

May (*cheerily, as though to naughty children*) You know what *I* think? I think you're not who you say you are.

She wags a finger at them as if to say I know your game and goes out

Angela rushes to Stan

Angela They know.
Stan Who know?
Angela My husband — your wife! (*She clings to him*)
Stan How you know they know?
Angela *She* knows.
Stan How she know?

Angela She just said … "I think you're not who you say you are" (*She breaks away from him. Dramatically*) No we're not … we're just two people deeply in love who don't want to cause pain to others … two people deeply in love and with nowhere to express that love other than in the back of an uninsured van and the last time we did I got covered in emulsion which is very hard to explain when I'm supposed to be doing advanced Spanish and so we come to other peoples homes — like this — in order that we may share a stolen moment in the privacy of someone else's four walls under the pretext of taking measurements.

Stan has listened to all this, straining hard to understand her rather rapid English. He attempts to repeat what she has said

Stan No we not. We two people deep in … whatever you say we deep in … but how she know?

Angela I don't know … my husband your wife — they're having us followed — (*the dawning of*) — that man who was here.

Stan Man?

Angela The one asking all the questions. (*She looks at the card*) Desmond Donohoe, Samson Home Security. He's a detective!

Desmond comes in carrying his case. He is having trouble controlling his mounting frustration

As soon as they see him, Angela and Stan turn to face the wall and will "take measurements" as:

Warren follows Desmond in, carrying his case

Warren The point I am trying to make is that you have cost me fifteen pounds. Ah!

Desmond Did you put a hand on me then?

Warren No.

Desmond I could swear I felt a hand on me.

Warren No

Desmond Because if you're looking for trouble let me tell you this … I am fully-trained and completely ambidextrous. (*He mimes a karate chop with his free hand, puts his case in that hand, mimes a second chop with the other hand*)

Warren, flinching, has shifted his contact lens. Angela and Stan move along the wall as though still measuring and go behind the french window curtains. Desmond slumps into the sofa

Desmond (*hand to forehead*) I'm sorry. I had no right to speak to you like that.

Warren (*hand to eye*) Don't worry about it. This is a stressful occupation.

Desmond Let me take you into my confidence.

Warren I think you already have done.

Desmond Even further. (*He beckons for Warren to sit next to him*) I think my marriage is going out of the window.

Warren Wardrobe — sorry, window — oh yes?

Desmond I have one last chance to save it.

Warren (*clapping him on the shoulder*) Take it

Desmond If I make one more sale before midnight tonight I become Salesman Of The Decade.

Warren Hey, that's great, man.

Desmond The prize that goes with it is an all-expenses paid holiday for two in Jamaica.

Warren I'm a small island man myself. Well my mum is.

Desmond You're getting my drift.

Warren Err …

Desmond That holiday could save my marriage. The sea, the sun, the sand … the romance.

Warren Right. *Right.*

Desmond Which is why I want you out of the way. So that I can save my marriage. So that *you* can save my marriage. You do want to save my marriage, don't you Warren?

Warren I do, yes.

Desmond Bugger off then. (*Suddenly shouting*) All of you!

There is a cry of fear from Angela behind the curtain

Desmond (*hand to head again*) I'm sorry.

Warren No, you're all emotional.

Desmond I am, I am. (*He shouts towards Stan and Angela*) Bugger off!

The curtain shakes fearfully. Desmond turns back to Warren, opens his mouth to speak, but then gets up and moves to pull back the curtain to reveal Stan and Angela. They are facing the wall, Stan with tape, Angela with notebook

Desmond Excuse me, but as the young man says, I'm under considerable strain. (*He pulls the curtains back and moves to sit, putting his head in his hand again*)

Warren The thing is, you see Desmond … and I hate to tell you this … but I don't think *either* of us is going to make a sale. I think the only reason we're here is she wants someone to talk to.

Desmond looks at him between his fingers as:

May comes in with a laden tea tray

May Well, this *is* nice (*She puts the tray down and moves to the curtains*) In case you change your mind there's a droppa port in the sideboard — that's continental, isn't it? (*And goes straight back to sit and arrange cups and saucers as:*)

Angela and Stan will quietly come out from behind the curtains, and move along, still facing the wall, as though still taking measurements, and:

May I know what I've been meaning to ask you ... when did Yul Brynner die?
Warren Pardon?
Desmond Someone to talk to? (*He stares at May as:*)
May What year was it?
Warren What year was it what sorry?
May When Yul Brynner died.
Warren Umm.
Angela Nineteen eighty-five.

The doorbell rings

May (*to Warren*) Answer that for me, will you dear, there's a good boy.

Warren goes out, taking his case

Desmond remains staring at May

May Are you sure, dear?
Angela Oh yes, I have a memory for these things.
Desmond When was the Battle of Hastings?
Angela 1066.
Desmond Mmm.
May Because I've been trying to work out if it was before or after Mrs Marchmont went. Mrs Marchmont at number 34.

Warren enters, holding a business card

Warren (*looking at the card*) Jilly Jordan, The Magical Sound Of The Musical Module.

Jilly comes in. She is in her early 40s, heavily made-up, immaculately dressed in a designer suit and carrying a designer case. She has large hair, large lips, is fanatically exercise-thin, and doesn't so much walk as totter on Minnie Mouse legs in very high heels

Jilly Dynamic Action Keyboards conveying the faithful reproduction and subtle nuance of the grand piano ... oh what a lovely room ... you must be Mrs Archer ... I love your hair, I bet you go to Leslie at Smile, sorry I'm late but I was sexually molested coming off the North Circular, if it hadn't been for that man exercising his greyhound I might still be lying in the gutter. This must be your lovely family, I can see you're so close, so close, you're so lucky to have a family, all I've got is my husband and he's confined to a wheelchair and seldom available.

From which we gather that she has had some very dodgy elocution lessons. The others have all been staring at her—except May who has been pouring milk. Now Warren snaps out of it with:

Warren Warren Wallis, The Wonderful World Of Wardrobes.
Desmond Desmond Donohoe, Samson Home Security. (*He shows his tie and socks*)
Stan Stankowski, Stanislaw, No Job Too Small.
Angela And assistant.

Cards are rapidly exchanged

May Isn't this nice? Just like the old days. Come and sit yourself down, dear, and I'll be mother.

Jilly sits on the sofa, next to Desmond. Warren quickly moves to sit next to her, so that she is sitting between them. She crosses her leg revealingly and smiles at Desmond and:

Jilly (*"whispering" to Desmond*) God, you're so attractive. (*She "whispers" to Warren*) You too.

And she puts a hand on each of their thighs. Stan and Angela lean over to have a look. Desmond and Warren simultaneously cross their legs

May Now then ... who takes sugar and who abstains?
Warren Ah!

CURTAIN

ACT II

The same. Moments later

The CURTAIN *rises. May is pouring tea*

May My hubby met him once, you know.
Others Who?
May Yul Brynner. He was sitting in a layby off the A11. Well he said he was Yul Brynner but you do, don't you? (*She holds up a cup*) There you are, dear.
Jilly What lovely cups. Are they Clarice Cliff?
May Weston-super-Mare, dear, the weekend he won the pools — sugar?
Jilly I shouldn't but I will.

May passes the sugar bowl. Warren takes it. Desmond takes up Jilly's teaspoon

Desmond How many?
Jilly I'll let you know when to stop. (*As she looks close into Desmond's eyes, she squeezes Warren's leg*)
Warren Ah!

Warren will hold the bowl and Desmond will spoon slowly, neither of them taking their eyes off her as Angela whispers to Stan

Stan May I have word?
May What's that, dear?
Stan You say we not who say we are.
May Who did?
Angela You did.
May Did I?
Jilly Stop.
Stan You say … (*to Angela*) ... what she say?

Angela whispers as:

Jilly It's very naughty I know but I succumb so easily.

Desmond nods blankly. Still in a daze

Stan You say ... we not who say we are.
May Oh yes, dear, so I did.

Angela gasps, grasps Stan

Stan Did?
May Well you can't be, can you? (*To the others, jokily*) They can't be, can they?
Others No.
Warren Can't be what? Ah!
Stan How can't?
May Have you ever known a workman not take a cup of tea when it's offered?
Others No.
May (*to Stan*) There you are, you see. *(To the others, still jokily)* Unless they've got trouble with their waterworks.
Others Yes.
May They can't *both* have trouble with their waterworks though, can they?
Others No.
May Our old postman used to have trouble with his waterworks. I said to him, look on the bright side I said ... the more you wee the less you cry.
Angela So when you said we're not who we say we are it was simply a jocular observation.
May I expect it was, dear, yes.
Stan Jocular observation?
Others A joke.
Stan Ah! Was ... "not who say you are ha-ha" not "not who say you are".
May Very similar, yes dear.
Stan Ah. Ah! (*He throws up both arms in triumph, then remembers that one of them is in a sling and brings them down quickly*)
May Oh well, perhaps I can persuade you to partake when you've finished.

Angela gasps, seizes Stan

Stan How you mean — finished?
May After you've done your bit of measuring.
Angela Oh measuring — yes — measuring. (*She shows everyone her notebook and pencil*)
Stan You say whole house.
May Whole house what, dear?
Stan Whole house paint paper.

May Did I really?
Stan I think gloss better. As long as it nice colour. Where you prefer we start
— upstairs or downstairs?
May I don't mind really. Downstairs. Then you can work your way up like
my son, my David.
Stan Your son painter?
May No dear, executive.
Stan OK. Commence foreplay in kitchen.

Stan and Angela go out hurriedly

May Now then: who'd like a nice biscuit?

*She passes the plate to Warren who holds it out for Jilly whose fingers flutter
over the plate as:*

Jilly I shouldn't really.
Warren ⎫
Desmond ⎭ *(together)* No?
Jilly But d'you know, nothing's passed my lips all day.
Warren ⎫
Desmond ⎭ *(together)* Oh?
Jilly And I can always work it off in the gym, can't I?
Warren ⎫
Desmond ⎭ *(together)* Yes.

She takes a biscuit and a ladylike nibble

Jilly Yummy. (*She runs her tongue round her lips to catch crumbs*)

Warren and Desmond remain entranced as:

May Did I hear you say you go to the gym, dear?
Jilly Three times a week min.
May What, you climb up wall bars and things, do you?
Jilly I do everything. I really like to punish my body. Go through the barrier.
May My hubby went through the barrier once. We was late for the train to
Margate. The fuss it caused, you would have thought he was Reggie Biggs
or something.
Desmond Ronnie.
Jilly That's me in a nutshell.
Warren Really?
Jilly I've always had such huge appetites. The psychiatrist said it was
because I was abandoned as a baby.

May What, they left you under a bush or something, did they dear?
Jilly I'd rather not talk about it, it still hurts, I'm afraid. (*She bravely stifles a tear*)
May It's amazing the things people throw out nowadays, isn't it? I found a fried egg on the pavement yesterday. Still warm and only one bite out of it.

Jilly has bravely recovered

Jilly (*to Warren*) I love your eyes. They're so different.
Warren Thank you.
Jilly I find a man with different eyes incredibly attractive.

Desmond touches his tie and re-crosses his legs in an attempt to draw her attention to his socks. She squeezes his leg

May Did I hear you say you were sexually assorted, dear?
Jilly Very nearly.
May Well that's not nice, is it?
Jilly It happens to me all the time. I don't know what it is. Men somehow seem to want to do the most terrible things to me.
Warren ⎤
Desmond ⎦ (*together*) No.
Jilly You're so sweet, so sweet, but yes, yes they do. There's something about me that seems to…excite them.
Warren ⎤
Desmond ⎦ (*together*) No.
Jilly I think it's because I'm so vulnerable (*And suddenly she is again on the verge of tears. She "bravely" stands up sharply, thrusting her cup at Warren and looks around the room with:*) I love this wallpaper. Is it William Morris? It is, isn't it, it's William Morris … (*To Desmond*) Do you like William Morris?
Desmond I love him.
Jilly Show me your socks again.

He raises his trousers

Jean Paul Gaultier, Spring Collection.
Desmond Desmond Donohoe, Samson Home Security.
Jilly You must be very strong (*She feels his biceps*) God yes (*She shivers*) Will you do something for me?
Desmond I will.
Jilly Will you come outside and help me in with my instrument?

Desmond I will.
Jilly *Will* you?
Desmond I will.

Jilly bends to May who has been sipping tea and staring at the soundless telly

Jilly I'm just going to bring my instrument in from the car and then we can
have a little demonstration.
May Oh that's nice, dear.
Jilly (*looking deeply into Desmond's eyes*) Are you really truly sure?
Desmond Always a pleasure, never a chore.

And, having completed their couplet, Jilly totters out followed by Desmond

May That's nice. I shall look forward to that, a little demonstration. (*She
sips her tea*) What's she demonstrating again?
Warren Oh no! (*He stands up, holding both cups, feet close together*)
May Oh no what, dear?
Warren I've lost my lens.
May Oo-er. Where do you think it's gone then?
Warren I don't know, it must be on the floor somewhere. Nobody move!
May Don't worry, dear, I'm bound to pick it up tomorrow when I do my bit
of hoovering.
Warren That's very nice of you but I shall need it to get home. (*He puts down
the cups, having groped uncertainly for the table on tiptoes, gets on his
knees and starts myopically searching the carpet*)

Stan comes in, his clothing somewhat dishevelled

Stan You want similar tile in kitchen?
May Oh I think so, don't you?

Stan makes to go, but:

Stan Is Muslim?
May Is what, dear?
Stan Is praying?
Warren Yes I am actually, praying I can find my lens.
May He's lost his lens. (*She points at her eye*)

Stan hesitates, then gets on his knees to assist

Stan What colour is lens?

Warren Excuse me, whatever colour it is, it's mine.

May You find all sorts of things in carpets. Wildlife, all sorts of things. There was this very interesting documentary on the telly. Do you know how high a flea can jump?

Warren ⎫ (*together*) No?
Stan ⎭

May Ten inches.

Stan Ten inches? (*Consulting his tape measure*) Is two hundred and twenty four millimetres!

May That's why social workers and policemen and vicars and such like wear wellington boots. When they visit houses where they know there are likely to be fleas. (*She sips her tea*)

Warren Why?

May Because they know fleas can only jump ten inches.

Stan What if flea sitting on picture rail?

May Don't ask me, dear, I'm a viewer not an expert. Wear a wellington hat, I suppose.

Jilly enters

Jilly Here I am, safe and sound, no mishaps!

Desmond backs into the room, carrying a plastic-covered keyboard, the other end of which is carried by Angela whose clothing is somewhat dishevelled

Where would you like me to put it? (*She playfully slaps Desmond's bum*) Naughty

May Oh I don't mind, dear, anywhere you fancy.

Jilly Umm ... (*finger to mouth*) ... what about ... on the table here. (*She moves across to the table*)

Desmond and Angela follow

Desmond On the table, on the table.

May You'll have to move my washing.

Jilly (*to Desmond*) We'll have it on the table then, shall we? (*And immediately puts a finger to his lips*) Naughty naughty naughty. (*She moves the washing basket*)

Desmond and Angela will put the keyboard on to the table as:

Jilly Telescopic legs are of course available as an optional extra.

May I wish you could have met my hubby. Now he *did* have legs. And oh how we danced! We loved our dancing. We came second you know in the East Acton All-comers Invitation Foxtrot and he'd only just had his new truss fitted. (*Of the television*) Oh I don't like this. I wish I could find my plunger.

The keyboard is now on the table

Jilly That's lovely. You're so sweet ... so sweet (*She blows a kiss and hands the washing to Desmond*) Now then … plug. (*She bends over a chair to unplug a table lamp*)

Angela moves to the crouching Stan

Angela I'm ready when you are, Mr Stankowski.
Stan One moment please.
Desmond What's going on?
Stan Lost lens. (*He mimes*)
Angela I shall be waiting — upstairs.

She shows her notebook to everyone and goes out

May I tell you what, dear — try these. (*She holds out her own glasses*)
Warren (*looking up myopically*) Pardon?
May Give him these, will you dear? (*She gives them to the kneeling Stan*)

Stan gives them to Warren who puts them on as:

Warren Thank you.

Jilly straightens up, holding the lamp

May Best pair of glasses I ever had, they are.
Jilly Did you go private?
May No, dear, found them on a bus. (*She gives Stan a playful little prod with her toe*) Still. No good to me if I can't find my plunger, are they?

Jilly gives Desmond the table lamp and bends over the chair again to plug in the keyboard. She has to stretch and one of her legs waves in the air. Desmond is transfixed by her bum

May How are they?

Warren, still on his knees, looks straight ahead. The [trick] glasses make his eyes look enormous

Warren They're a bit strong, actually.
May That's all right, dear, it was the same with me: you've got to give them the chance to adjudicate.

Desmond drags his eyes away from Jilly's bum and moves across to Warren, gets on his knees, still holding the washing and lamp, and:

Desmond (*a "hiss"*) Don't think I don't know what you're up to.
Warren (*staring blindly*) Pardon?
Desmond There's me trying to give you some pointers and there's you knowing every trick in the book.
Warren Pardon?
Desmond All this Blind Pew stuff ... it's just an attention-getting device. Page twenty-three, "Selling For Beginners".
Warren What about your socks?
Desmond At least they're my own.
Warren I *had* to put them on.
Desmond Oh yes?
Warren She would have been offended otherwise and it's page twenty-seven.
Desmond That's what I mean ... every trick in the book. Well we'll see about that ….
Stan Ah! (*He holds up the remote control which he found under the sofa*)

Desmond snatches it and shoves it into a pocket as:

Desmond Now where were we, auntie?
Warren I told you ... she doesn't really want to buy anything.
Desmond And I told *you*…she's *got* to.
Stan Where assistant?
May Waiting for you upstairs.
Stan Ah. Continue estimate. (*He goes to the door*) No job too small.

He goes

Desmond (*brightly*) Auntie.
May Yes, dear.
Desmond How would you like to see and hear who is knocking at your door without having to move from the comfort of your favourite armchair?
May That sounds very nice, dear, yes.
Desmond I'll go further: how would you like to see and hear what is going on not only outside but in every room in the house and without moving a muscle?

May I don't know dear but my hubby would have loved it.

Desmond He would he would ... and so will you ... because what we are talking about, auntie, what we are talking about ... is the Cyclops Three Thousand! (*He puts down the basket and lamp and triumphantly holds up his case*)

Jilly Won't be a jiffy

Desmond I know what you want to ask me, you want to ask me how it works. Well go ahead: ask me.

May Ask you what, dear?

Desmond How it works.

May How does it work?

Desmond A very intelligent question. Simply by turning your television into a one hundred percent secure security system — and how does it do that?

Warren ⎫ (*together*) No?
Jilly ⎭

Desmond By the use of one Cyclops power supply unit and as many high-resolution fully-adjustable pan and tilt fully-weatherproof response cameras as you decide upon, all incorporating a mini-microphone and a built-in anti-condensation heater and all conforming to British Standards six seven nine nine class seven.

Warren ⎫ (*together*) Wow!
Jilly ⎭

Desmond (*triumphantly*) What do you say to that, auntie?

May Does it have a plunger?

Desmond As many as you like.

Angela (*off*) Stan! Stan!

May I tell you what.

Desmond What's that, auntie?

May I've just had a really good thought.

Desmond You couldn't share it with a more understanding fellah.

May He might have swallowed it.

Jilly Ah!

May You might have swallowed it dear.

Warren (*blindly*) Pardon?

Jilly takes the plastic cover off the keyboard

May Your eye. It might have dropped in your cup of tea and you might have drunk it.

Warren Oh no!

Desmond (*hands to head*) Oh no.

May Only one way to find out ... have a look in your cup.

Warren stands, groping, in the glasses

Warren Which one is mine?
May I don't know, dear, you'll have to experiment.

Warren will grope around to collect the tray and weave his way out as:

Jilly turns on the keyboard which is illuminated with variously coloured flashing lights

Desmond What I'm going to do, auntie, is give you a practical demonstration.
May Excuse me dear but I think I'm already getting one.

Jilly plays a dramatic chord on the keyboard. Throughout the following, Desmond will open his case and, moving around on hands and knees, will take a small control box round the back of the television and twiddle

May Oh I say!
Jilly (*her vowels are even more tortured when she does her sales pitch*) Dynamic Action Keyboards convey the faithful reproduction and subtle nuance ... oh, I've done that, excuse I ... let me present to you the keyboard where man meets machine. More than ten months of in-depth research and development have enabled us to open up a whole new world of musical expression and creativity. (*She presses a button*)

There is a burst of "The Birdie Song"

May Oh I say!
Jilly Furthermore, the TW600 incorporates the exclusive facility of the two thousand five hundred Your Most Popular tunes memory bank. Name that tune and the TW600 will lay down your baseline!

A brief fanfare from the keyboard

Desmond Right. All done. What I'll do now, auntie, is slip outside and set up a couple of cameras — just temporarily and with no obligation.
May That's all right, dear, as long as you don't strain yourself.

He takes up his case and makes to go out. Jilly stops him, looks close into his eyes and, with the sexy edge she always uses when selling to males:

Jilly With six sliders and four buttons the TW600 is the perfect choice where size and ease of handling are of paramount consideration.
Desmond (*holding up his case*) Make this sale and I'll consider *anything*.

She gasps and pulls him closer

Jilly Might *you* be interested in one of my instruments?
Desmond *Anything.*
Jilly God, I love short legs and a stocky trunk. I was once engaged to a
Welshman, you know.
Desmond I don't wish to be offensive but I'm a desperate man.

He goes out

(*Off*) Desperate!
May I think he might have prostrate trouble.
Jilly I think you might be right.
May My sister had a bunion, you know. She said I'm going to see that Dr
Maynard and I said you don't want to see Dr Maynard, he's mental, you
want to see Dr Lloyd-Owen, *he's* feet and she said oo, little Miss Knowall
and I said I may not know much but one thing you cannot fault me on is
my intimate knowledge of the National Health Service.

There's a bang from upstairs

Angela (*off*) Stan! Stan!
Stan (*off*) Angela! Angela!
Jilly With six sliders and four buttons the TW600 is the perfect choice where
… oh no I've done that, excuse I … so … I tap in the title and away we go.
May Lovely.
Jilly What would you like?
May Well since you mention it, dear, I wouldn't mind a bar of fruit and nut.
Jilly By way of a favourite melody.
May How about … (*singing*) "Mares eat oats and does eat oats and little
lambs eat ivy"
Jilly How do you spell it?
May How about White Christmas?

Jilly taps quickly at the keyboard with:

Jilly W … H …

Warren comes in. He points to his eye

Warren Found it, thank you. (*He hands May her glasses*) Thank you.
May Sit down, dear, we're having a bit of a concert.
Jilly And it's one two three and ...

We get a snatch of a conventional version of White Christmas

Or at the flick of a switch ——

A brief snatch of a rap version of it

Or even ——

A brief snatch of a Handel version

Hours of family fun at easy terms spread over a five year period.

Warren's mobile rings

Warren Excuse me. Hello? (*To May*) It's my boss.
May Oo-er.

Warren will move away, and speak quietly into the mobile, his back turned away, as:

Jilly has remained stock-still, like a switched-off robot. She always goes into this mode when her sales patter is interrupted. But now she comes back to life with:

Jilly But before we move on to financial considerations, I know you'll want to know more and quite rightly too about the rich and vibrant tones of the TW600 as created by our worldwide team of keyboard sampling specialists.

Her mobile phone gives a frenetic musical burst

Excuse I. (*She speaks into the mobile*) Jilly Jordan. (*Listening and using lots of body language*) That's very naughty. Yes I know. Stop it. Yes I will you know I will I promised. I can't, not now, not just like that. Because people are listening and besides, I'm demonstrating. No. *No.* Oh all right then you know you're irresistible but only if you promise to place an order. You promise? You really truly promise? All right then — *you* start. (*She listens, making oh-oh-oh little noises, and:*)You are so naughty. (*To May*) I'm really really sorry but it's a very important client, not that you're not important of course you are but he's an accountant in North Finchley and needs to speak to me urgently about my spreadsheet.
May Off you go then, dear.
Jilly Two tickys, promise.

She totters out, already back to the call

Go on then … naughty.

Warren has finished his call

May No offence but she looks half-starved to me. Like that young woman who's just moved in across at number seventy-three.
Warren (*his mind elsewhere*) Yes?
May She's supposed to be a ballet dancer and according to Mr Patel she lives on nothing but goats milk and orgasmic cauliflower. She has it specially deported from Italy.

Through the window, we see Jilly appear in the garden, using her mobile with its built-in camera to make great use of body language

Warren Mr Mason — that's my boss said that if it would help you make up your mind he's prepared to offer a further thirty percent discount.

Jilly is going through the motions of a telephone orgasm, holding out the phone so that the caller can see it on camera

May I wonder if she'd fancy a nice sausage sandwich or something.
Warren But the thing is …
May Something with a decent bit of meat in it.
Warren The thing is …

Desmond comes in, case in hand

Desmond I thought I'd quickly put in a couple upstairs — just by way of demonstration and with no obligation — what would you say to that, auntie?
May Whatever you think best, dear.
Desmond Then all I'll have to do is the back here and we're all set.

He indicates the french window outside which Jilly is reaching simulated climax. She moves out of sight, yes yes yes-ing!

May Lovely.

Desmond goes out, singing "I'm Only A Strolling Vagabond"

May He's a real sprucer, that one. Mind you, he's got a lovely voice. My sister couldn't sing for toffee, you know. I think that's why she was so jealous of me, me getting a solo spot in the school choir and her only being third reserve in the netball team.

Warren Excuse me but … you're not really interested, are you?
May Interested in what, dear?
Warren I mean I understand, at least I think I do, and I don't mind, I mean not me personally, I mean it's all experience as far as I'm concerned and I don't want to be rude or anything but I don't think you really..I mean I don't think …

Jilly totters in dramatically

Jilly … I'm so sorry I'm so sorry but some of my clients are so demanding.
May That's all right, dear, you're a businesswoman.
Jilly Quite honestly I'm often treated more like a servant.
May I was a Nippy once, you know. At Lyons. That's how I met my hubby: he was delivering bacon.
Jilly Some of them would have me on my knees all day.
May My sister was a school cook, you know.
Jilly I think that is so brave, so brave.
May Her custard was a bit lumpy but her suet pudding was wonderful. You could feel your heart slowing down as you eat it.

Desmond comes in, slapping his hands

Desmond Well then, auntie, that's the front and the upstairs done and how long did it take me, no time at all no time at all … so then, just the back and it's time to rock and roll … (*To Warren*) Give me a hand, will you, I can't reach.
Warren Excuse me, I'm in wardrobes.
Desmond (*hissing close*) Don't push it.

He goes out. Warren reluctantly goes after him

Jilly How do you feel then?
May In what way, dear?
Jilly About the TW600 (*She gives a little burst of "I Love A Piano"*)
May I tell you what, dear — I like your outfit.
Jilly (*delightedly*) Do you?
May I got married in an outfit like that. With a little fox fur and his mother complaining about the venue. That's what I mean: stay where you are and it all comes round again.

Warren appears at the french windows. He is weaving under the weight of Desmond who, still holding his case, is perched on Warren's shoulders. All we can see of Desmond is his lower half and the case. Warren comes to a stop facing the windows, and remains unsteadily, as the case goes up out of sight

Jilly (*posing*) It's the first time I've worn it.
May Oh yes?
Jilly It's DKNY. I love DKNY, don't you?
May To be quite honest I prefer ITV.
Jilly D'you like the shoes?
May Very nice dear.
Jilly Jimmy Choo.
May Bless you.
Jilly In terms of comfort I would have preferred something a little less elevated but the truth is I can only think clearly in high heels.
May My hubby did his best thinking in his shed. He used to go down there and come back totally exhausted. I *wish* I could find my plunger. (*She moves around, looking for it as:*)
Jilly Can I let you into a little secret?
May Oh yes, I love secrets.
Jilly (*confidentially*) I don't buy new.
May No?
Jilly Oh no, I couldn't afford it. (*Even more confidentially*) I go to this private shop in SW7 ... Seconds From The Stars ... MaxMara, Gucci, Joseph, all the top labels ... would you like to come with me one afternoon?
May Thankseversomuch, dear, but I'm dedicated to Marks.

Desmond giddyups Warren who weaves them out of sight

Jilly Not that I want you to get wrong idea. Underneath it all I'm just a working girl doing her best in a very competitive market to support a seriously-damaged husband.
May What part of him is it?
Jilly From the waist down and spreading.
May What happened?
Jilly We were on an errand of mercy and the brakes failed. I was thrown clear but my husband, who only that very morning had been made redundant, had to be cut out by two firemen and a sheet metal worker.
May They say things often come in threes, don't they?
Jilly (*on the verge of tears*) If only we'd had children.
May They can do wonders nowadays, even from the waist down.
Jilly (*feigning hope*) D'you really think so?
May Oh yes, it was on Holby City. Or was it the other one?

Desmond comes in, carrying his case, followed by Warren who is dabbing his eye with a handkerchief. Desmond sets down the case and:

Desmond Right then, auntie. What I'm going to do now is go outside and knock at the front door whereupon I would like you to go immediately to Channel Six.

He holds out the remote control and mimes clicking it at the television

May There it is!
Desmond Can you do that for me now, auntie?
May (*taking the control*) Oh yes, dear, according to my son it's the one thing I *can* do.
Desmond (*pointing to the screen*) I'll see you later, in full closeup. But until then … (*Singing*) "Goodnight pretty lady, goo-ood night."

Desmond makes to go out, but is intercepted by Jilly

Jilly It's not just the money. It's giving my sick child the chance of a new kidney.

Desmond goes

May points the control at the television, ready for the off. Warren, still with his hand to his eye, moves to Jilly

Warren (*quietly*) Might I have a word?
Jilly I'd love to but I'm about to resume my demonstration.
Warren That's what I wanted to talk to you about, actually.

She gasps

Jilly You've got such lovely sensitive hands. Are you by any chance considering a keyboard?

There is a loud knock at the front door. May immediately presses the control

May (*pointing at the television*) It's him!
Desmond (*on the television*) Hello, auntie.
May Doesn't he look natural?
Desmond (*on the television*) Are you receiving me?
May (*to the screen*) You do, you look really natural. Hello, he's gone. (*She points the control at screen, pressing all the buttons*)
Jilly (*to Warren, gazing into his good eye*) I'm not a career salesperson, you know
Warren I don't think *I* am.
Jilly I'm only doing it to support my aged mother.
Warren I thought you said you were an orphan.
Jilly We were re-united.
May Was it Jerry Springer?

Jilly I believe it was, yes.
May He's wonderful, that man, wonderful.

Desmond comes in

Desmond Did you receive me, auntie?
May I did and you looked really natural.
Desmond What I'm going to do now is put in a similar appearance round the back — channel number seven — have you got that, auntie?
May Channel number seven. (*She points the control at the television intently*)
Desmond You're a joy to do business with. (*A "whisper" to Warren*) Bugger off.

Desmond goes out, passing Stan coming in, looking even more dishevelled

Stan Now estimate master bedroom requiring complete concentration and lack of interruption. Thank you.

He goes out

Desmond appears at the french window. He waves

May points at the television

May (*thrilled*) Oh look, he's waving. (*She waves back at the screen*)

Desmond says something, unheard

(*To the screen*) Sorry dear you'll have to speak up.

Desmond tries again

It's no good, I think the sound's gone. (*She enunciates at the screen*) ...
I say I think the sound's gone. (*She points the control at the screen, pressing buttons like mad*)

Desmond, with growing irritability says, unheard "Press the sound button"

Pardon?

Desmond mouths, pointing ... "Press the sound button"

Pardon?

Desmond (*voice-over: over-loud and clear*) Press the bloody button!
May Well that's charming I must say. (*She points the control in an attempt to change channels*)

Desmond moves out of sight

Jilly (*to Warren*) Might you really be interested in a TW600?
Warren I think they're very good, yes.
Jilly Oh look ... (*She drops to her knees*) A twenty pound note ... (*She remains on her knees*) You must have dropped it.

His fingers twitch but:

Warren I don't think so, thank you.

Desmond comes in, going straight to May

Desmond As you will have seen, auntie, the Cyclops Three Thousand detects all unwanted callers or canvassers.
May Pardon me but you swore.
Desmond Only by way of demonstrating the undesirable element that comes aknock-knock-knocking.
May My hubby used to swear. Mind you, he never raised a hand to me. He seldom raised anything else come to think of it.
Desmond You might also have noted that the wide-angled lens provides panoramic views not only of your doorstep but also of your garden, your boundary walls and your garage.
Warren She hasn't got a garage.
Desmond She's got a wardrobe though and she doesn't want another one — bugger off! (*Straight back to May*) Furthermore, recordings from the Cyclops Three Thousand are accepted by the police as admissible evidence should an intrusion occur.
Warren (*to Jilly*) She doesn't want one. She doesn't want *anything*.

There is a crash from upstairs

Angela (*off*) Oh Stan ... Stan!
Stan (*off*) Angela, Angela!
Desmond Imagine it, auntie ...
May What's that, dear?
Desmond You're sitting here ... all alone ... watching your favourite television programme ... suddenly you hear a strange noise ...

Jilly, caught up in the drama, plays a sting from "Psycho"

Is it the wind?

Jilly plays a sting of wind effect

Is it a scavenging animal?

Jilly plays a sting of an elephant trumpeting

Sorry.

A sting of a wolf howling

You panic … your heart pounds …

A throbbing heartbeat

… am I imagining things? But no — there it is again.

The "Psycho" sting

But this time, you remember … you are not alone … you have your Cyclops Three Thousand (*He points the control at the screen*) You look at your front door. Nothing.

Musical sting

You look at your back door. Nothing.

A slightly bigger sting

You look in your bathroom. Nothing.

A slightly bigger sting

You look in your bedroom ... (*He opens his mouth to say "nothing" as:*)

Jilly makes to play a chord … but instead they all lean into the screen as we hear:

Angela (*voice-over*) Oh Stan…Stan…
Stan (*voice-over; in Polish*) I love you I need you I want you.
Angela (*voice-over*) Oh Stan….Stan!
Stan (*voice-over*) Angela…Angela!

Jilly Is that Janet Reger she's wearing? I love Janet Reger, don't you?

Warren turns away, covering his good eye

Stan (*voice-over, in Polish*) I'm going to make you my own!
Angela (*voice-over*) Oh Stan ... Stan! (*But a complete change of tone as:*) Stan ... what's that on top of the wardrobe?
Warren (*uncovering his eye*) What wardrobe?
Angela (*voice-over*) Up there ... that little black box.
Stan (*voice-over*) Is hat box.
May I haven't got a hat box. I haven't got a hat. (*She waves at the screen*) Coo-ee!
Angela (*voice-over*) It's a camera!
Desmond The Cyclops Three Thousand.
Stan (*voice-over*) Camera?
Angela (*voice-over*) A camera — we're being filmed! (*She screams*)

Everyone's head turns as they try and keep up with the falling camera

May What's happened to the picture?
Desmond What's happened to my camera?

 He goes out as:

May bangs on the television set

Warren Excuse me.

 He follows Desmond out

Jilly Mrs Archer.
May Yes, dear?
Jilly How would you like to singalong your own choir?
Stan (*voice-over*) Open door!
Angela (*voice-over*) Go away, I hate you!
May I'll singalonga anything, dear, especially if the telly doesn't work.
Warren (*trying to draw attention to upstairs*) Excuse me ...
Jilly And what is more, you need never sing alone. At the touch of one finger you will have full augmented choral backing ... be it classical.

A burst of "Hallelujah!"

    Liverpool.

A burst of "Yeah Yeah Yeah"

Ethnic.

A burst of Indian singers

Or similarly esoteric.

A burst of Highland Reelers

Stan has come in

Jilly You name it, the TW600 provides it.
Stan Polish?
Jilly Polish is in the pipeline.

Desmond comes in, staring down at the twisted remains of his little black camera

Desmond My camera, my lovely little camera.
Stan Excuse.
May Yes, dear.
Stan Have slight problem

There is a burst of hammering and screaming from upstairs. It stops as suddenly as it starts

May What problem's that, dear?
Stan (*to Warren*) Need help with ladder for consult assistant.
Warren Me?
May Give him a hand, there's a good boy.
Stan Thank you.

Stan goes out

Warren Yes but I'm wardrobes.

He goes out after Stan, Desmond thrusting the ruined camera into his hands as he goes

Desmond moves towards May, writing on the back of one of his cards as:

Desmond Auntie.

May Yes, dear.

Desmond Since you are rated as an A1 property, and since I now regard you more as family than client, I am prepared to release our premium protection system at the all-time once and once only special price of ... (*He holds the card out for her*)

Jilly tries to peep, but he gets in the way

Desmond What do you say to that, auntie?

May I wish I could find my glasses.

Desmond's mobile rings. He is torn between answering it and continuing his sales thrust

Desmond Desmond Donohoe. (*His face and voice change*) Laura ... you're what? Don't say that, Laura, don't say that ... (*He drops to his knees, turned away from us, and will plead into his mobile as:*)

Jilly Don't let it influence you in any way, but every morning I wake up and it's a struggle.

May My hubby always used to say you can't beat a good dose of salts.

Jilly Mentally I mean.

May Oh, mentally. Can't help you there, dear. Mind you, you get some very interesting articles in the TV Times. Dr Wassisname.

Warren appears at the french windows, under the weight of Stan's ladder which he will set up uncertainly as:

Jilly Oh God. So much pain ... so many disappointments. (*Confidentially, of Desmond*) Be very careful before you sign anything. (*And*) Not that I'm bitter but why is it that life is so hard for me and so easy for other people?

There is a loud burst of banging and screaming from upstairs followed by the sound of Desmond sobbing into his mobile

Desmond One last chance ... I'm begging you, Laura, I'm begging you ... (*His sobbing intensifies*)

May nudges Jilly

May (*confidentially*) I think he's upset.

Jilly (*confidentially*) Selling For Beginners, page ninety-seven, The Last Resort. Take my advice and ignore him.

Desmond sobs louder

May I tell you what, dear, I wonder if he'd like a bit of a sing-song, cheer himself up a bit?

Stan comes in, looking for Warren. He sees him outside, gives a little "Ah" and makes to go out again but:

Do you know any nice songs, do you, dear?

Stan looks at her. Then takes off his cap and launches into a doom-laden Polish lament. He gets to the end of the first line but May stops him continuing with:

May No dear no, something with a bit of life in it. Some Barry Manilow or something.

There is a burst of screaming from upstairs

Stan (*shouting at the door*) How many more times? Two hundred and sixty-five centimetres plus VAT!

He goes out

Desmond has remained on his knees, his phone hand lifelessly at his side, his shoulders heaving. Now he pulls himself together, gets up and moves to May as though nothing has happened, with:

Desmond I've just had a word with my marketing director who is prepared to throw in an electronic peephole completely free of charge.

Throughout the following, Stan will appear at the french windows and climb the ladder which is held vaguely steady by Warren who gets a foot in his face for his trouble

Jilly Excuse I but we were just about to dip into the memory bank. Two Thousand Five Hundred of your Most Popular Tunes.

Desmond I know what you're thinking, auntie, you're thinking much as I'd love the Cyclops Three Thousand, it's just that little bit outside my range. Well then, let's have a look and see what we can do. (*He whips out a pocket calculator and starts pumping away as:*)

Desmond Two point three-seven divided by forty-nine over six …

Jilly (*of the keyboard*) Name that tune! (*She gives a burst of music*)

May nudges Desmond, upsetting his calculations

May We thought we'd have a bit of a singsong, dear.

Jilly Augmented by the magical tones of the TW600!

Desmond (*to May, an aside*) Be very careful before you sign anything. (*And*) I've just had another look at my figures and I'm prepared to throw in a Sony Walkman and unlimited supply of cassettes for when you go jogging — what d'you say to that, auntie?

May I wish my hubby was here, he could have done his Sheik of Araby.

Jilly Is that sheik as in desert or chic as in Harvey Nicks?

May Arabs, dear. Rudolph Valentino.

Jilly (*gasping*) Valentino! (*And she taps into the keyboard as:*) S ... H ... E ... I...

Desmond ... is that what you'd like auntie? Is that what will make you happy?

May What's that, dear?

Desmond has taken up a pillow case from the washing basket. He puts in on his head, arab-wise, and poses with eyes narrowed, mouth sneering, hands on hips. He laughs arrogantly

May (*pointing excitedly*) It's him, it's Rudolph!

Desmond And it's one two three four ...

And the keyboard strikes up and Desmond sings the first verse of "The Sheik of Araby". He takes May's hand and guides her to her feet

During the following, Stan will descend the ladder with (dummy) Angela draped over his shoulder. Warren will attempt to guide him down and get another foot in his face for his trouble

   Stan carries Angela out of sight

Warren realizes that his lens has gone and will grope around outside the window, looking for it

May sings the second verse

Desmond has guided her across to his metal case which he tips over with a toe and indicates for her to hop on to it. Which she does. She will tap dance as he kneels and looks up at her proudly, sheikwise ... and Jilly, not to be outdone, takes a tea towel from the basket and covers the lower part of her face and waves her arms over her head, concubinewise ...

   And Warren will find his lens and move out of sight, putting it back in as:

May and Desmond sing the rest of the song

  At the end of the number, Stan carries Angela in

Desmond and Jilly are each side of May, each with outstretched hands holding a pen and a piece of paper

May There now, wasn't that nice! What shall we do next?
Jilly
Desmond | *(together)* Sign here.
May What's this?
Jilly
Desmond | *(together)* The contract.
May Oh I don't sign things.

Warren comes in, handkerchief to eye

  Do I, dear?
Warren Pardon?
May I don't sign things, do I?
Warren *(generally)* That's what I've been trying to tell you.
Others What is?
Warren She doesn't want anything. Do you?

A slight moment. May moves to sit

May No. No I don't.

There is a collective gasp from everyone. Stan puts Angela down as:

May has remained looking straight ahead, suddenly a frail little lady

May I know what you all think. You think I'm just a silly old woman.

Desmond makes to say something but Jilly puts a hand over his mouth

Warren No we don't.
May Oh I think you do, dear: and more than silly … you think I'm stupid.
Warren No.
May I don't blame you. People always have. Even my own son. He thinks I'm so stupid I don't know that he's lying, that he doesn't *want* to come and see me. And when he does put it an appearance, he doesn't say anything,

he just sits here and tells me how tired he is and sometimes I want to scream
but I daren't because then I'd never see him so I make him a cup of tea and
I watch my television and ... enjoy other peoples' lives, even if they are
only made of soap. And he says that's nice, I've come all this way and all
you do is watch the television, well then I might as well go and he does and
in a way I don't mind because then he can blame me and ... he's got a lot
on his plate and ... well he is my son, isn't he, he is my flesh and blood. I'd
go and see *them* but you know when you're not really welcome, don't you?
So what happens is, I sometimes don't speak to a living soul for days —
well, neighbours aren't what they were, are they? — so when one of you
nice people phones up ... I know it's wrong of me, I know you've got your
living to make but ... the thing is, you see ... not knowing much ... being
stupid ... doesn't mean to say you don't ... doesn't mean to say ... (*She
trails off and for a moment it looks as if she might cry. But she gives a brave
little smile and:*) Still. I shall be dead soon and out of everybody's way.
But until that merciful day I shall continue to depend, as I have depended
these last long and lonely years ... on the kindness of unsolicited callers.
(*She reaches out a hand*)

*Warren gives her his handkerchief. She blows her nose into it and hands it
back to him. This moment. The little old lady surrounded by the cruel world.
Then Jilly moves to the keyboard and strikes a note and:*

*Warren sings "My Yiddisher Mama". The others "herumm" and join in so
that they become a close harmony mostly-humming group conducted by
Jilly. The humming continues under as Warren moves sit next to May and:*

Warren May I say that that was one of the most moving speeches I have ever
heard and I include Kevin Keegan.

Singing/humming

May Thank you, dear.

Singing/humming

Warren And what is more I know it came straight from your heart.
May No, dear, no ... (*She produces a book from down the side of the chair*)
... "Buying For Beginners", Chapter Ten, "Avoiding The Hard Sell" —
only mum's the word, eh? We don't want to upset them, do we? (*She
shoves the book back in its hiding-place*)

*Warren stares at her, then stands and provides the last long and decorative
note to the song. Desmond, still with the pillowcase on his head, moves to
take May's hand and:*

Desmond I've learned a great lesson tonight.

May What's that, dear?

Desmond That you can deceive others but that you can never deceive yourself.

Warren Tell it like it is, man!

Desmond How could I have deceived myself into believing that two weeks in Jamaica all expenses paid would have saved a marriage that had died long ago?

May I tell you what would though, dear.

Desmond (*full of hope*) What's that?

May The faithful reproduction and subtle nuance of a TW600.

Desmond Of course!

Jilly shoves her order form at him and he happily signs about six copies as:

Jilly (*to May*) You've made me so happy.

May Are you sure, dear?

Jilly You're right. How can I be happy when every night I have to leave my crippled husband alone and unprotected?

May Has he got one of those monitors above his bed that goes beep beep beep like it does in Casualty?

Jilly He has yes.

May The Samson Home Security Cyclops Three Thousand would turn that monitor into a one hundred per cent secure security system.

Jilly (*gasping*) You're right!

May And with a minor modification to his plunger he would be able to see and hear into every room without so much as moving a muscle.

Jilly He can't move a muscle.

May Then you're looking at a thirty per cent discount.

Desmond Forty! (*He thrusts his order pad at Jilly*)

Jilly (*as in her simulated orgasm*) Yes ... yes … yes!

Angela For us too, the deception ends here! I am not his assistant! (*She tosses away the glasses and proudly tosses her luxurious hair*)

May I know you … you're that part-time manager from the dry cleaners' … (*She nudges Desmond*) They've got a special offer on this week if you're thinking of getting those socks dyed.

Stan Have further announcement.

Angela Stan and I have been lying to each other. Neither of us is married.

There are gasps from the others

Stan Only say married for fear commitment.

Angela (*to May*) But thanks to you, we now realise how much we mean to each other.

Others Ah
Angela We've decided to run away together, haven't we, Stan?
Stan We are going to live with my people!
May What part of Poland are you from, dear?
Stan My people in Shepherds Bush!
Others Ah.
May I tell you what though ——
Stan ⎫ (*together*) What?
Angela ⎭
May — if you're going to live together, you'll be needing somewhere to hang your clothes
Others A wardrobe!
Warren My first sale!

The others applaud

Warren And listen ... (*he mouths an "ah" but there is no sound*) ... I've lost my nervous tic.
May Yes, I know, dear, it went about half an hour ago.
Warren How can I thank you?

There is a loud knock at the front door

May You can go and see who that is for me, there's a good boy.

Warren makes to go but:

Desmond One moment! (*He points the remote control at the television*)
Man's Voice (*from the television*) Good-evening, Mrs Archer. You asked me to call ... Kenneth Crowhurst of Persimmon Portable Trampolines.
Others Persimmon Portable Trampolines?
May I thought a bit of exercise might do me good. Let him in while I make us all a nice cup of tea, will you, dear?
Desmond Auntie auntie auntie ... you can't go jumping up and down.
Stan Not on trampoline.
Angela No disrespect but ...
Jilly A lady of your age.
Warren You could hurt yourself.
May Yes I suppose I could really. Mind you ... my sister couldn't do this for toffee.

And she does a handstand, her ankles supported by Stan, or the slow splits, or a tricky tap dance step, or any sort of unlikely physical party piece

Warren Ah!

FURNITURE AND PROPERTY LIST

ACT I

On stage: Sofa
Armchairs. *By* **May**'s *chair*: TV remote control. *In chair*: pair of
National Health spectacles, second pair with trick lenses
Sideboard. *On it*: photograph of man collecting a diploma
Table propped up on furniture catalogue. *On it*: telephone, lamp
Large television set
Very new document case containing apple, part-eaten sandwich, bottle
of water, steel tape measure, notepad, ballpoint pen and catalogue
for **Warren**

Off stage: **Desmond**'s business card (**Warren**)
Silver metal case containing small control box and order pad (**Desmond**)
Plastic basket full of washing including pillowcase and tea towel
(**Desmond**)
Handbag containing five-pound note (**May**)
Packet of biscuits and change (**Warren**)
Laden tea tray (**May**)
Jilly's business card (**Warren**)
Designer case containing order forms (**Jilly**)

Personal: **Desmond**: mobile telephone, tiny tape recorder, ID card and photograph,
business cards, pocket calculator, watch (worn throughout)
Warren: mobile telephone, business cards, ten-pound note,
handkerchief
Stan: business cards, steel tape measure
Angela: notebook and pencil
Jilly: business cards, twenty-pound note

ACT II

Off stage: Plastic-covered keyboard—possibly practical, with variously-coloured
flashing lights (**Desmond** and **Angela**)
Twisted remains of little black camera (**Desmond**)
Ladder (**Warren**)
Dummy **Angela** (**Stan**)

LIGHTING PLOT

Practical fittings required: television flicker effect, flashing lights on keyboard
One interior with exterior backing beyond french windows. The same throughout

ACT I

To open: General interior lighting with early evening effect on exterior backing;
flicker effect from television

No cues

ACT II

To open: General interior lighting with early evening effect on exterior backing;
flicker effect from television

Cue 1   **Jilly** turns on the keyboard   (Page 38)
            Flashing lights on keyboard

EFFECTS PLOT

ACT I

Cue 1   **May**: " … about her internals."   (Page 5)
          Brisk ring at doorbell

Cue 2   **May** points the remote control at the television   (Page 5)
          Soap opera soundtrack (See note on copyright, p.64)

Cue 3   **Desmond** uses the remote control   (Page 13)
          Fade soap opera soundtrack

Cue 4   **May**: " … a very thin nib, I can tell you."   (Page 18)
          Ring at doorbell

Cue 5   **Desmond**: "May I see it, please?"   (Page 19)
          Ring at doorbell

Cue 6   **Angela**: "Nineteen eighty-five."   (Page 27)
          Ring at doorbell

ACT II

If a keyboard is available that can make the sounds and effects required and the actor playing Jilly can play the instrument, the sound plot for the keyboard can be performed "live"; if not, the effects below can come from a recorded source.

Cue 7   **Jilly** plays the keyboard   (Page 38)
          Dramatic chord

Cue 8   **Jilly** presses a button   (Page 38)
          Burst of "The Birdie Song"

Cue 9   **Jilly** presses a button   (Page 39)
          Brief fanfare

Cue 10   **May**: ' " … National Health Service". '   (Page 39)
          Bang from upstairs

Cue 11   **Jilly** flicks a switch   (Page 39)
          Snatch of a conventional version of "White Christmas"

Cue 12   **Jilly** flicks a switch   (Page 39)
            Snatch of a rap version of "White Christmas"

Cue 13   **Jilly** flicks a switch   (Page 39)
            Snatch of a Handel version of "White Christmas"

Cue 14   **Jilly**: " … over a five-year period."   (Page 40)
            Warren's mobile rings

Cue 15   **Jilly**: " … keyboard sampling specialists."   (Page 40)
            Frenetic musical burst from Jilly's phone

Cue 16   **May**: "It's him!"   (Page 44)
            Desmond's voice from TV; dialogue as p.44

Cue 17   **May**: "Doesn't he look natural?"   (Page 44)
            Desmond's *voice from TV; dialogue as p.44*

Cue 18   **May**: "Pardon?"   (Page 45)
            Desmond's *voice from TV; dialogue as p.46*

Cue 19   **Warren**: "She doesn't want anything."   (Page 46)
            Crash from upstairs

Cue 20   **Jilly** plays the keyboard   (Page 46)
            Sting from "Psycho"

Cue 21   **Jilly** plays the keyboard   (Page 47)
            Sting of wind effect

Cue 22   **Jilly** plays the keyboard   (Page 47)
            Sting of elephant trumpeting

Cue 23   **Jilly** plays the keyboard   (Page 47)
            Sting of wolf howling

Cue 24   **Jilly** plays the keyboard   (Page 47)
            Throbbing heartbeat

Cue 25   **Jilly** plays the keyboard   (Page 47)
            Sting from "Psycho"

Cue 26   **Jilly** plays the keyboard   (Page 47)
            Musical sting

Cue 27   **Jilly** plays the keyboard   (Page 47)
            A slightly bigger sting

Cue 28   **Jilly** plays the keyboard   (Page 49)
              A slightly bigger sting

Cue 29   **Jilly** makes to play a chord   (Page 47)
              Angela's *and* **Stan**'s *voices from television; dialogue as p.47*

Cue 30   **Warren** turns away   (Page 48)
              Angela's *and* **Stan**'s *voices from television; dialogue as p.48*

Cue 31   **May**: "Coo-ee!"   (Page 48)
              Angela's *voice from television; dialogue as p.48*

Cue 32   **Desmond**: "The Cyclops Three Thousand."   (Page 48)
              Angela's *and* **Stan**'s *voices from television;*
              dialogue as p.48, ending with a scream
              and the thud of a falling camera

Cue 33   **Jilly** flicks a switch   (Page 48)
              Burst of "Hallelujah!"

Cue 34   **Jilly** flicks a switch   (Page 48)
              Burst of "Yeah Yeah Yeah!"

Cue 35   **Jilly** flicks a switch   (Page 49)
              Burst of Indian singers

Cue 36   **Jilly** flicks a switch   (Page 49)
              Burst of Highland Reelers

Cue 37   **Stan**: "Have slight problem."   (Page 49)
              Hammering and screaming from upstairs

Cue 38   **May**: "I wish I could find my glasses."   (Page 50)
              Desmond's *mobile rings*

Cue 39   **Jilly**: "... so easy for other people?"   (Page 50)
              Loud burst of banging and screaming from upstairs

Cue 40   **Jilly** presses a button   (Page 52)
              "The Sheik of Araby" plays

Cue 41   **Jilly** strikes a note   (Page 54)
              Note from keyboard

Cue 42   **Desmond** points the remote control   (Page 56)
              Man's voice from television; dialogue as p. 56

COPYRIGHT MUSIC

A licence issued by Samuel French Ltd to perform this play does not include permission to use the Incidental music specified in this copy. Where the place of performance is already licensed by the PERFORMING RIGHT SOCIETY a return of the music used must be made to them. If the place of performance is not so licensed then application should be made to the PERFORMING RIGHT SOCIETY, 29-33 Berners Street, London W1T 4AB.

A separate and additional licence from PHONOGRAPHIC PERFORMANCES LTD, 1 Upper James Street, London W1R 3HG is needed whenever commercial recordings are used.

SOAP OPERA SOUNDTRACK

Permission must be sought from the broadcaster if a recording is to be used of any TV programme.

Lightning Source UK Ltd.
Milton Keynes UK
UKOW06f1026290716

279502UK00001B/79/P